May the [illegible] peace an His always, Julia Mack

God's very special People

Tate Publishing
& Enterprises

God's Very Special People: An Activity Book for Children Who Grieve

Cover design and illustration by Melissa Griggs
Layout design by Kristen Polson

Published in the United States of America

ISBN: 1-5988658-5-4
06.10.19

God's very special People

An Activity Book for Children Who Grieve

JULIA MACK

Tate Publishing & *Enterprises*

Dedication

I dedicate this book to the memory of my grandparents and my nephew, Marty Bunte, whom God has chosen as His very special people and taken to heaven.

Acknowledgements

I would like to acknowledge Ryan and Eric Swanson, who as youngsters in 1990, lost their father to a sudden heart attack. Their grief and the lack of available material to support grieving children first inspired the creation of this work.

Thank you to my husband, David, for his support of this project. A big thanks goes to my sister-in-law, Lisa Mack, for her encouragement which ignited the process of getting published. I also thank my parents, Richard and Beverly Wehling, for my Christian upbringing and for lessons taught in learning to acknowledge and meet the needs of others.

Preface

A bag of colored candies is required for this activity. You may want to purchase additional bags of candy if you have more than one grieving child. Give the child the package of candy. Adults with preschoolers, please have the child follow the instructions as *you* read each page. Insert the dearly departed's name in each blank. After completing this exercise, encourage the child to color each of the faces. Having the child review the theme will reinforce the concepts within.

Introduction

Hopefully, this game with candies will allow you to see a little better why God has chosen to take ____________ (i.e.: Nana Bea, Marty) to heaven at this time. I know you will miss him/her *a lot!*

Just remember, God needs ___________ (i.e.: grandma, cousins) in heaven too.

Open the bag of candy.

Pour all of the candies on the table.

Decide which color is your **favorite** color of candy.

Separate your favorite color candies from the rest of the candy.

Think of the candies as all the different people in the world. And think of the separate, favorite color candies as **very special** people.

Imagine **God** has separated people instead of you separating candies.

Look at the special color candies as if they were very special people whom God had chosen as *extra* kind, loving souls whom He couldn't wait any longer to bring to heaven.

God wants His very special people closer to Him right now.

God has looked at their hearts and seen *all* the love they have for Jesus. Because they love God so much and God loves them so much—God brings them to be closer to Him.

God wants His very special people to share all their kindness and love with the other **souls in heaven.** There they can be healthy and happy and spend the entire day, everyday, making God feel joyful and loved.

Look at the big pile of candies. They don't look the same without the special color candies with them. They look like **something's missing.**

Imagine the big pile of candies as you and your family without ______________. Your family will look **different** without him/her.

Things won't be the same. But different isn't all bad. You can feel good knowing you still have each other.

And it doesn't mean that you forget about God's very special people. You should **hold onto your memories** and all the good times you had together.

You can be happy knowing there are little souls in heaven that ___________ can read to, or sing and play games with.

Mix all the candies back up.

Eat all the candies, because you know they really aren't people. We were just pretending.

Never forget,

____

is one of God's
very special people!

Cut out and use these **finger puppets** for roll playing to include your very special person. Ask questions such as:

- Are you closer to God?
- Is everyone kind in heaven?
- Are you healthy?
- Do you miss me?
- Are you happy in heaven?

(fold)

(fold)

(fold)

(fold)

(fold)

TATE PUBLISHING & *Enterprises*

Tate Publishing is committed to excellence in the publishing industry. Our staff of highly trained professionals, including editors, graphic designers, and marketing personnel, work together to produce the very finest books available. The company reflects the philosophy established by the founders, based on Psalms 68:11,

"THE LORD GAVE THE WORD AND GREAT WAS THE COMPANY OF THOSE WHO PUBLISHED IT."

If you would like further information, please call
1.888.361.9473
or visit our website
www.tatepublishing.com

TATE PUBLISHING & *Enterprises*, LLC
127 E. Trade Center Terrace
Mustang, Oklahoma 73064 USA